"I'm Sorry," Said Denny

by

Sallie B. Gigliotti

AuthorHouse™
1663 Liberty Drive
Bloomington, IN 47403
www.authorhouse.com
Phone: 833-262-8899

Because of the dynamic nature of the Internet, any web addresses or links contained in this book may have changed since publication and may no longer be valid. The views expressed in this work are solely those of the author and do not necessarily reflect the views of the publisher, and the publisher hereby disclaims any responsibility for them.

Any people depicted in stock imagery provided by Getty Images are models, and such images are being used for illustrative purposes only. Certain stock imagery © Getty Images.

This book is printed on acid-free paper.

ISBN: 978-1-4343-9999-1 (sc)

Library of Congress Control Number: 2008909834

Print information available on the last page.

Published by AuthorHouse 08/27/2022

authorHOUSE

Bebe the Butterfly spent most of her summer days soaring through the air enjoying the sun. She only stopped so she could play with her friends, Denny, the new neighborhood deer, and Ms. Bouncy the Bunny, who had lived in the same meadow since she was a baby. Denny had moved into the same meadow as Ms. Bouncy this past spring.

Today was just like the others for Bebe the Butterfly. She woke up, went to the daffodil field across the street for a bite to eat, and then was off to visit her friends. It was the same as yesterday—until she rounded the trees to the meadow.

What she saw was a terrible sight. Ms. Bouncy was hopping and jumping around as if something had really upset her. Then Bebe the butterfly saw that Denny the Deer had his back turned, and he was eating the only patch of green grass left in the meadow.

Bebe arrived just as Ms. Bouncy started to cry. "What's wrong, Ms. Bouncy?" asked Bebe. Thru her tears, Ms. Bouncy replied, "It's Denny. He came over to my patch of grass this morning, and, without asking, he began eating it, and now it's almost all gone."

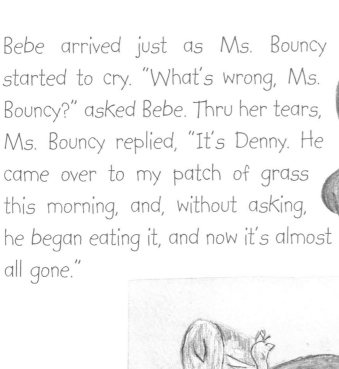

Bebe landed on the ground in front of her upset friend and looked up at her. Bebe's beautiful yellow and black wings glimmered in the morning sun and made Ms. Bouncy feel just a little bit better, but she still had no breakfast because Denny was eating all of it.

Then Bebe flew off and landed atop Denny's back. Bebe asked him, "Did you ask if Ms. Bouncy would mind sharing her grassy meadow with you? She has been living and eating here for years, and there is not much grass left, and now you have eaten it all."

"No, I didn't ask. I thought she knew that since I moved in, I would be eating here too. If I didn't eat here, I would have to walk across the field to the old farm for breakfast. I didn't think Ms. Bouncy would mind," responded Denny as he bent down for another mouth full of grass.

Bebe remembered how she felt when her feelings were hurt and started to feel sad for Ms. Bouncy. Bebe sat and thought hard about what Denny could do to make his friend feel better. "Ah ha!" she yelled. She had an idea!

She quickly spread her wings and flew down to the ground so she could be face to face with Denny. He looked at her, clearly sad that he had hurt his friend's feelings. Bebe quickly told him her idea. She said, "All you have to do is say you are sorry for eating her grass. That way she will know that you did not mean to hurt her feelings."

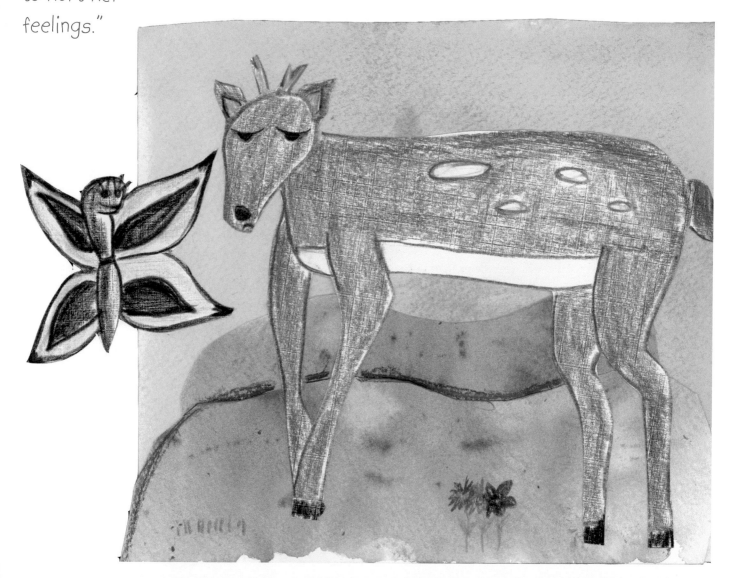

Denny thought that was a great idea. He quickly ran over to the tree where Ms. Bouncy was still sitting and sobbing. He lay down beside her so she could see his face. He looked straight at his bunny friend and said, "I'm sorry. I didn't mean to hurt you. It's my fault that you don't have breakfast because I ate all the grass." Ms. Bouncy looked up with a sparkle in her eyes, feeling happy at what her friend had just said.

"It's okay," she said. "But now we don't have any grass to eat until it grows back."

"I have an idea," said Denny as he stood up. "I can go to the farm to get us food until our grassy meadow grows back. It won't take long, and it's the least I can do since I ate all of the grass."

Ms. Bouncy smiled and began to hop around the tree. "That sounds great," she exclaimed. "Then we will both have food!" With that, Denny walked off to go get his first load of food for him and his good friend Ms. Bouncy. Bebe landed on his back as he started on his journey.

"See how apologizing fixed everything? Now, we are all friends again. After you finish bringing the food over, we can all play this afternoon," said Bebe. Denny looked up at his fluttery friend, smiled, and said, "I can't wait!"

Sallie B. Gigliotti grew up in rural Virginia and currently lives near Reading, Pennsylvania with her husband Anthony, and their two young sons Gabriel

and Joshua. She received her Bachelor's in Marketing from Virginia Commonwealth University in 2002. After spending several years in corporate America, she is currently a stay at home mother.

Her vision for this book is to show the importance of manners to children by helping them build self respect and to show respect for others. "I'm Sorry," said Denny is the first of an upcoming series of children's book by Sallie Gigliotti. Look for future books by Sallie focusing on even more mannerisms.